Fred Rogers: The Life and Legacy o
Neighbo

By Charles River Editors

About Charles River Editors

Charles River Editors is a boutique digital publishing company, specializing in bringing history back to life with educational and engaging books on a wide range of topics. Keep up to date with our new and free offerings with this 5 second sign up on our weekly mailing list, and visit Our Kindle Author Page to see other recently published Kindle titles.

We make these books for you and always want to know our readers' opinions, so we encourage you to leave reviews and look forward to publishing new and exciting titles each week.

Introduction

Derek Wolfgram's picture of Rogers in 1994

Fred Rogers

"This is what I give. I give an expression of care every day to each child, to help him realize that he is unique. I end the program by saying, 'You've made this day a special day, by just your being you. There's no person in the whole world like you; and I like you just the way you are.' And I feel that if we in public television can only make it clear that feelings are mentionable and manageable, we will have done a great service for mental health." – Fred Rogers

An anomalous YouTube video crudely entitled "Mr. Rogers is a [sic] Evil Man" stands at over 1.8 million views, with 1,000 likes and a whopping 30,000 dislikes. Similarly, saying an ill word about the universally adored Mister Rogers on the forums of the imageboard, 4Chan, will get the commenter torn to shreds by even its notoriously toxic anonymous users, and almost definitely ousted from the online community for good. In an age where even the motives of Gandhi and Mother Teresa are questioned by the cynical and they are at times vilified as "frauds," one would be hard-pressed to find a rational argument against the untouchable character of Mister Rogers.

When one does happen upon such an abnormality, the public is quick to defend the gentle soul. "It takes a special kind of scum to hate Mister Rogers," reads the top comment on the aforementioned video, posted by user Sergei Ivanovich Mosin. The video has been picked apart by multiple journalists from the likes of Huffington Post and the Pittsburgh Magazine, amongst many others.

So who exactly was Fred Rogers, and how did the host of one of history's most beloved shows win the hearts of children around the world? *Fred Rogers: The Life and Legacy of the Legend behind Mister Rogers' Neighborhood* profiles one of America's most iconic television personalities. Along with pictures of important people, places, and events, you will learn about Fred Rogers like never before.

A Diamond in the Rough

"Knowing that we can be loved exactly as we are gives us all the best opportunity for growing into the healthiest of people." – attributed to Fred Rogers

Perhaps it is the treasury of heartwarming stories surrounding Mister Rogers that continues to preserve his pristine reputation to this day. One such story, for instance, tells of Rogers en route to a meeting in New York. With no cabs in sight and the tick of his watch pulsating in his ears, the man and his crew ducked into the subway and swiftly filed into a carriage, anxiously bouncing their legs. The late party kept to themselves, huddled by a corner, and spoke in hushed tones.

The 5:00 p.m. rush hour meant that every square inch of the carriage was occupied, allowing them to blend in seamlessly with the other riders, or so they thought. A pack of schoolchildren returning home from school spotted him, but rather than heckle or accost him for autographs, the kids swayed back and forth, sweetly singing to him the theme song of his iconic children's show: "It's a Beautiful Day in *Mister Rogers' Neighborhood.*" It wasn't just the children either, as grown folks, many of whom had watched him as children themselves, joined the impromptu choir, serenading the beaming, twinkling-eyed man.

Another story comes from one of his interns, known only as Lisa, whose fondest memory involved Rogers during a trip to Boston sometime in the late 1980s. Rogers and his entourage were due for a glamorous party at the luxurious mansion of an unnamed PBS executive. When Billy, the limousine driver, asked Rogers what time he was expected to return, the puzzled Rogers replied, "Why, where are you going?" Following a lovely evening, Rogers moved up to the passenger's seat, listening intently and laughing heartily as an ecstatic Billy chattered away about his life. The night did not end there. Rogers then suggested that they stop by Billy's home, so he could meet the wonderful folks that had bred such a stand-up young man. The intern recalled, "So, there we all are, getting out of a limo in the middle of West Roxbury, Massachusetts...We walk in the door, and there's Billy's dad coming down the stairs in his bathrobe, a cigarette dangling from his lips. He takes one look at Fred and yells, 'Holy [expletive]! You're Mister Rogers!'" The place soon erupted into happy bedlam as Billy's neighbors poured into the formerly quiet suburban home, bearing with them trays of fresh cookies and treats. Rogers promptly took over the piano, tickling the ivories as the crowd around him belted along to the jaunty tunes. Needless to say, it was a beautiful memory Billy and his family forever held dear to their hearts, but so did Rogers, who proceeded to send Billy's family a Christmas card every year after that. Rogers also took time out of his hectic schedule to ring up Billy years later when he learned that Billy had been diagnosed with AIDS.

The anecdote (or in this case, urban legend) that best encapsulates the public's love and respect for Rogers is one reported by the March 1990 issue of *TV Guide.* There are two versions of this tale, one pertaining to Rogers' *Oldsmobile* sedan and another to his battered, decades-old *Impala.*

As these stories go, Rogers was either at work, or babysitting his grandson, when his vehicle was stolen. News of the grand theft auto, given its victim, spread like butter, and was soon swiped up and broadcasted by every medium of media. In less than 48 hours, Rogers awoke to find his otherwise undisturbed car parked neatly by the curb in front of his house. The note clipped under the windshield wipers read, "If we'd known it was yours, we never would have taken it."

Rogers, his employees insist, was born with the gift of relating to everyone, no matter the age or walk of life. There were no desks in his office, but rather, a comfortable couch and matching armchairs, for he considered a desk an unnecessary "barrier" between him and his staff. The soft-spoken and affable man was also the kind of employer who rented out the whole amusement park in his hometown for a day every summer for the children of his employees.

Rogers' compassion, assert millions of children around the globe, was truly unparalleled, turning him into a virtually infallible figure whom the most dramatic say humanity does not deserve. His viewers have grown accustomed to his slow and soothing cadence, and his habit of spelling out each and every one of his actions to his audience. It was only years later that a fan revealed the reason behind Rogers' actions; early on in his show, he had received a letter from a blind 8-year-old fan named Katie. "Please say when you are feeding your fish, because I worry about them," the young girl pleaded. "I can't see if you are feeding them, so please say you are feeding them out loud." From then on, he made certain to tweak his narrations, rounding them out with more descriptions not only for Katie, but for all the blind boys and girls potentially tuned into his show.

These are only a handful of the numberless uplifting and soul-stirring stories inspired by the sweater-sporting luminary. Even more mystifying is his disarmingly reserved, unassuming, and, dare one say, borderline "boring" demeanor. With his crisp, peppered side-part and single-color cardigans, the wildest thing about him seemed to be changing patterns of his neckties and bow ties. The man was backed only by a simple set, cheap props, and his limitless wisdom – no kooky hats, fancy tricks, or gimmicks – yet the grandfatherly figure managed to captivate and find his way into the hearts of generations upon generations of children, inadvertently setting a standard that has yet to be surpassed.

So, how did this mere mortal of a man come to be perceived as anything but, and why does this unlikely children's television mogul continue to be so relevant today, close to two decades after his death?

On the 20th of March, 1928, James Hillis and Nancy McFeely Rogers, a well-heeled couple from the industrial town of Latrobe, Pennsylvania, welcomed their first and only biological son. The devout Presbyterian couple christened their pride and joy after Nancy's father, naming him Fred McFeely Rogers. James, the breadwinner of the family, was an eminent entrepreneur who began as a tool and dye manufacturer, and eventually rose to prominence as the president of the prosperous McFeely Brick Company. Nancy, the cultured and well-educated daughter of

Frederick Brooks McFeely, was a dedicated housewife and mother often seen at charity drives, bake sales, and other community gatherings as both patroness and volunteer. Suffice it to say, the young, hazel-eyed tyke grew up comfortably and well-fed in the spacious 3-story home of James and Nancy Rogers on Weldon Street, complete with manicured lawn and a troop of hired help.

Fred only later learned to fully appreciate his many blessings, for he not only lived in comfort and moderate luxury, he was raised in a loving household. He remained an only child until the age of 11, when James and Nancy brought home his adopted 1-year-old sister, Nancy Elaine. The kindly couple also took in and became the foster parents of an orphaned African-American teenager by the name of George Allen, the son of their loyal housekeeper.

Though Fred regarded George as blood, as he did Elaine, George also served as his personal chauffeur, which Fred himself was never too keen about. Fred later recounted, "When I was 3, this young man was just an early teenager, and his mother had died. And my mom and dad said, 'Come live with us.' He turned out to be a real model for me. As a matter of fact, when I was in high school, he taught me how to fly [a Piper Club plane]." George was an intrepid soul who rose above the era's prejudices and silenced his disparagers with his accomplishments. As Fred noted, "And right after that, he went to teach at Tuskegee Institute in Alabama and taught all the black fliers in the country to fly in the Second World War...I really admire him."

Fred's preliminary schooling began at Jane and Juliet Robb's kindergarten, in the parlor-turned-classroom of the sisters' cottage by Kingston Dam, before he moved on to receive his formal education at a local public school. Even then, the childhood friends he had noticed something strikingly different in the little boy's character. According to Peggy Moberg, Fred's carpool buddy, classmate, and neighbor, Fred was imaginative, intelligent, and engaging, but he lacked the urges to roughhouse and tackle the playground like the "typical" boy, so he had trouble fitting in with his classmates. During the weekends, Peggy accompanied Fred – who often ate alone, owing to his parents' figuratively full plates – for lunch, prepared for them by the Rogers' personal chef. After lunch, the pair scampered up the stairs and into Fred's playroom on the 3rd floor, lavishly furnished with heaps of dolls, stuffed animals, marionettes, puppets, and decked out doll houses and homemade puppet theaters, which the generous boy never hesitated to share with his visitors.

While Fred loved his mother dearly, he admitted that her overprotective qualities were at times difficult to bear. The crime rate in the sleepy town of Latrobe, which lay about 3 hours away from the state capital, was among the lowest in the region, a community populated by mostly well-to-do Christian families and small-business owners. The town's most intriguing landmark at the time was the original factory of the Rolling Rock Beer Company, famed for their distinctive, clover-green draft cans and "pony" bottles.

That said, Nancy's paranoia was somewhat understandable, for the national media in the mid-1930s aggressively sensationalized the tragic kidnapping of Charles Augustus Lindbergh, Jr., the toddler son of one of America's most famous men. Fred was prohibited from leaving the house on his own, even in broad daylight, and was later placed under the supervision and care of his foster brother, George.

Inevitably, Nancy's overprotecting nature contributed to her son's unpopularity. The painfully shy and mostly friendless child reconciled his loneliness with organ playing, which he was introduced to by his grandmother, who gifted him a polished, brand-new piano at the age of 5. The sorrow and wrath Fred and other children of the era had to repress were alleviated by the calming melodies that wafted out of the instrument. Said one of his oldest friends, "[Fred] could just laugh or weep through the tips of his fingers."

Fred later went on to find solace in the companionship of his brother and sister. George often shared meals and chatted with Fred, offering the young one advice and, more importantly, sensitivity and understanding. After completing his homework, George drove Fred and Elaine to the cinema, and the siblings were especially partial to campy 1930s-esque musicals. The naturally rhythmic lad not only lost himself in the movie magic, he absorbed the tunes from the soundtrack almost effortlessly, so much so that he was able to play them by memory on his own piano just hours later.

When unaccompanied, the inventive Fred sought support from his inanimate friends, his prized puppet collection. The pudgy and asthmatic child was often unwell, and as such, spent much of his free time – including the entirety of one summer due to a terrible spell of hay fever – cooped up in his bedroom, as per his panicky mother's instructions. He did his best to fill the void of isolation in his heart with his stringed companions, but the anxious and bullied boy remained helplessly forsaken. "I used to cry to myself when I was alone...I was the perfect target for ridicule," Fred admitted. "And I would cry through my fingers and make up songs on the piano."

The torment from his peers only seemed to worsen with age. Amy Hollingsworth, author of *The Simple Faith of Mister Rogers*, relates how bullies chased him home after school. "We're going to get you, Fat Freddy!" hollered the wicked boys as a fully-flushed and frightened Fred sprinted to his porch as quickly as his stubby legs would carry him. Fred remembered, "I resented the teasing. I resented the pain. I resented those kids for not seeing beyond my fatness or shyness."

Though the harassment he suffered was partly responsible for the benevolent and deeply considerate man he would one day become, the older and wiser Fred was not one to dwell on bad times. He chose instead to pay tribute to the few, but radiantly bright stars he was fortunate enough to be blessed with during one of the most trying periods in his life. One such star was his grandfather, Frederick. Frederick's namesake frequented his farm, located just outside of Latrobe, and young Fred continued to visit him every winter after the elderly man eventually relocated to Florida to live out the rest of his retirement. The boy felt most secure when with his grandfather, for Frederick, an outwardly gruff "man's man" of a farmer, had a golden heart and unabashedly accepted the "unconventional" young boy as he was. The doting grandfather kept an eye on Fred from the sidelines as the boy played with the farm animals and cavorted about the countryside. Frederick urged his grandson to pursue his love of puppetry and to play his music as he pleased. Frederick also doubled as buffer of sorts against his occasionally overbearing daughter, waving off his frantic daughter affectionately whenever Fred attempted anything she deemed dangerous, such as riding a horse or climbing the stone wall on his grandfather's farm. "So the boy wants to climb stone walls?" said Frederick. "Then let the boy climb stone walls! He has to learn to do things for himself.""I climbed that wall," Fred later recollected with a wistful smile. "And then I ran on it. I will never forget that day."

Fred rarely asked for material gifts, but Frederick spoiled his grandchildren with mountains of presents, such as a 2-story playhouse constructed from scratch and an actual boat, rewarded to Fred for his stellar grades. As an adult, Fred nostalgically recalled the merry times his family – Frederick and at times, estate staff included – sung show tunes and gospel songs into the night by the crackling campfire as Nancy and Fred played duets harmoniously on the piano.

Fred's passion for music only continued to blossom. As a teenager, he graduated to the electric organ, and kept a thick file of his compositions. By the time he completed high school, he had written over 150 original pieces.

Frederick's endless empathy, admirable patience, and loving acceptance of those around him, regardless of creed or background, were values he consciously instilled in his grandson. While the other adults around Fred sympathized with the child's social quandaries, they advised him to conform to the antiquated norms so that "nobody [would] bother [him]." This, in turn, bothered the emotional young man, for he wished not to change his ways. Instead, he longed for "someone to tell him that it was okay to feel that way...[that] it was okay to feel bad about what happened, and even to feel sad..."

Frederick not only embodied the resilient and altruistic individual Fred aspired to become, he seemed to be the only one who accepted him without demur, and he convinced his grandson that there was nothing wrong with wearing his heart on his sleeve. Of all the meaningful conversations his grandfather had with Fred, there were some particular words that left a lasting imprint on him: "You know, you made this day a really special day. Just by being yourself. There's only one person in the world like you. And I happen to like you just the way you are." These words were hardly Shakespearean, but the uncomplicated, yet profound message it bore became the core tenet of Fred's future work. Fred later explained, "When I was a boy, I used to think that strong meant having big muscles, great physical power; but the longer I live, the more I realize that real strength has much more to do with what is not seen. Real strength has to do with helping others."

Fred also found unexpected friends among his neighbors, predominantly the charming, motherly women who lived on his block. One was a widow he called "Mrs. Stewart," whose home he sometimes took refuge in when the bullies came charging after him. Another was a friendly, hospitable woman he referred to as "Mama Bell Frampton." He thoroughly cherished all the times Mama Bell invited him in for "toast sticks," a piece of toast sliced into 4 pieces and livened up with a dollop of butter or fruit jam. "Seems like a simple thing," said Fred. "But 65 years later, I can still feel it – that neighbor's trust and my own pride at having made those first ones on my own. I think [Mama Bell] really did love me. She just somehow sensed what I needed to grow."

As easily distraught as Nancy tended to be, the metaphorical harness she fitted upon her children ultimately came from a place of love. She loved her children equally, made an effort to attend all school events, and did her best to cheer up her children with jokes, happy stories, or her vibrant singing voice. She made a splendid celebration out of every birthday, anniversary, holiday, and milestone, but she would not make a fuss about her own, and she crafted each of her presents by hand. She especially loved to knit, so much so that each and every one of the cardigans Fred wore on his show was knitted by Nancy.

Rudi Riet's picture of a sweater worn by Rogers now at the Smithsonian's Museum of American History

Nancy's thoughtfulness was paired with a striking ability to locate silver linings in the darkest and murkiest of clouds, a trait she had inherited from her own father. Whenever Fred became disillusioned or upset by the horrendous news of war, strife, or other harsh realities on the radio and television, his mother placed a consoling hand on his shoulder and gave it a tight squeeze. "Look for the helpers," she reminded him. "You will always find people helping. No matter how bad things are, there are always people who are helping."

Fred's social life remained relatively turbulent until his junior year, when he crossed paths with one of the most well-liked kids in Latrobe High School, a powerfully built jock by the name of Jim Stumbaugh. The 16-year-old Fred had shed most of his baby fat and was now a lanky, sharply-dressed teenager, his thick head of gelled hair parted neatly to one side, but the quiet, studious boy, a member of the school band and Camera Club, was still mostly ostracized by his peers. This all changed when Jim suffered an awkward landing and shattered his leg, rendering him bedridden in the hospital. That same afternoon, Jim, who had never spoken to Fred prior to this point, was visited by this very classmate, who brought with him Jim's schoolbooks and a list of the day's assignments, unprompted.

During Fred's 50th high school reunion, he described in a speech how Jim aided him through this rough patch in his life. "There [Jim was], probably the best-known, smartest, most active person in our class, and he welcomed me day after day. And what's more, he seemed to want to get to know me. I learned to trust him and told him some of my deepest feelings...By the time he got out of the hospital and back to school, he was telling all of his friends that 'that Rogers kid is OK'... he quietly included me in everything he thought I'd like."

With his peers retiring their preconceptions about him, Fred finally felt confident enough to let down his guard and explore his potential to the fullest extent. By senior year, Fred, a straight-edge, but non-judgmental vegetarian who distanced himself from cigarettes, booze, and other vices, had won over his peers, which he attributed to Jim, the one person "who believed in [him] and wasn't afraid to say so." Fred became more visible on campus - he was elected both student council president and editor-in-chief of the yearbook committee, and he was inducted to the *Quill and Scroll*, an international journalism society reserved for honor students. He braved several public speaking competitions and even bagged himself a trophy for the Kiwanis Extemporaneous Speaking Contest with his oratorical piece entitled "The U.N.O (United Nations Organization) is the Answer to a World Organization for Peace."

Fred was always supremely grateful about the rapport he established with Jim. "Little did I know that it would be the beginning of a lifelong friendship." Not even the most dazzling flashes of his impending celebrity could blind him from the memory of Jim Stumbaugh. When Fred learned that Jim had been diagnosed with an incurable illness decades later, he suspended all his plans at once and traveled to North Carolina to be with his dear friend.

A Calling

"We live in a world in which we need to share responsibility. It's easy to say, 'It's not my child, not my community, not my world, not my problem.' Then there are those who see the need and respond. I consider those people my heroes." – attributed to Fred Rogers

Following his graduation from Latrobe High School in 1946, 18-year-old Fred was admitted to Dartmouth College, one of the prestigious Ivy League 8, where he pursued a degree in Romance languages. Here, he remained for 2 years, but feeling unfulfilled, he made the pivotal decision to quest after the one passion that hauled him out of bed every morning: music. Thus, Fred accumulated his credits and transferred to Rollins College, based in the city of Winter Park, Florida, and majored in Music Composition.

Though he worked diligently to maintain his quality grades, the liberal-minded, college-aged Fred, a staunch proponent of equal rights and societal progress, became a familiar face at feminist and pro-equality rallies. About a year into his academic career at Rollins, he joined (and later captained) the Interfaith and Race Relations Committee (IRRC).

In many ways, the 1940s hinted at change for the cruelly oppressed African-American residents of the United States. Richard Wright, for one, became the first African-American to publish a bestselling novel with his gripping masterpiece, *Native Son*. Hattie McDaniel became the first African-American in history to win an Oscar for her supporting role as "Mammy" in the critically-acclaimed *Gone With the Wind* in 1939.

However, there was still plenty of restrictions in place. The talented and articulate Hattie remained well-employed throughout the better part of her life, but she was restricted to minor and subordinate roles, as evidenced by the 74 maid credits under her belt. Furthermore, though Hattie was awarded the coveted gilded trophy, she would have been banned from the premises had it not been for the multiple strings pulled by producer David Selznick. Even then, the stunning Hattie, who arrived in a resplendent turquoise gown embellished with rhinestones, was made to squeeze into a cramped table in the back of the room.

The long-awaited, but snail-paced change was also exhibited in the South. The Jim Crow institutions in Winter Park, which were erected to aid and cater to the needs of the African-American population, were grossly understaffed, financially deficient, and on the verge of collapse. The all-black community of Eatonville, about a 12-minute drive from Winter Park, was also in dire need of funding. As such, the IRRC chose to concentrate their efforts on these towns.

Members of the small, yet spirited committee were vocal advocates of civil rights, but rather than partake in the fiery protests cropping up across the country, the IRRC opted for a more "paternalistic," back-seat approach. They journeyed to and conducted research on these impoverished institutions and communities, and organized several fundraisers geared towards renovating and improving the living standards of these neglected residents.

Fred later penned a paper that illustrated the committee's accomplishments, and though the words may be cringe-inducing today, they were very much in line with the majority of even the "radical reformers" during the time. Furthermore, Fred may have personally condemned the segregation laws, but he, along with the members of the IRRC board, felt it more productive to work with, rather than against the questionable system. Once dismissed from their lectures, members of the committee boarded a public bus and zipped over to Eatonville, where they tutored students from an all-black institution called the "Robert Hungerford Normal and Industrial School." The committee, as reported by Fred, endeavored to click with the children outside of the classroom, too, including one instance wherein they "treated 96 colored kiddies to ice cream and cake for their Thanksgiving Party...at the Colored Day Nursery." The IRRC also donated a shipment of fluorescent lights to replace the busted bulbs in a town library exclusive to African-Americans, and hustled around town collecting funds for an all-black nursing home that would double as a hospital clinic.

In spite of the IRRC's ventures, many have criticized Fred for his omission of the NAACP in his report, and for his failure to acknowledge the cataclysmic racial violence that plagued the divided nation. On top of the committee's lack of a relationship with the NAACP, some arraigned them for their silence during the infamous 1949 Groveland kidnap and rape case, which saw 4 innocent African-American men revoltingly robbed of their lives and dignities. But at the end of the day, these compelling points aside, one must not diminish the good attempted by the IRRC, for Fred's revival of the committee was a triumph in its own right. Just a year before Fred's transfer, the Rollins student council unanimously voted to scrap a football game against the Ohio Wesleyan University for no other reason than the rival school's roster, which included Kenneth Woodward, an African-American running back.

Like every other university student, Fred's relationships and interactions with his professors differed. "I had a professor who did his best to scare everyone in his class," Fred later recounted. "And he gave me the lowest grade that I ever had in any school anywhere." Nonetheless, his less-than-palatable experiences with this unidentified instructor did little to taint his pleasant university years. He was resolved to stay the course, and his efforts in all classes remained solid. In the same breath, the respect the inquisitive Fred held for his teachers remained unaltered. He discovered a fatherly figure, adviser, and confidante in Dr. George Dimitrov of the Astronomy Department. "[Dimitrov always] looked for and found what was best in each of his students," said Fred. "When I look at the night sky, I still think of that extra-special, kind man."

Now that Fred had outgrown his inhibitions and was well on track to fully embracing himself as he was, his college years were marked by plenty of gaiety, mirth, and a cache of delightful memories. But the brightest highlight of his college years, bar none, was when he met an energetic and charismatic 20-year-old student named Sara Joanne Byrd. Sara, a native of Jacksonville, was the daughter of Ebra Edwards and Wyatt Adolphus Byrd, a well-schooled jack-of-all-trades who worked as a teacher, door-to-door salesman, and postal worker. When she, a music major herself, learned that Rollins was expecting a transfer student in the spring of 1948, Sara, who was eager to meet another student who shared her love for music, pounced on the sign-up sheet of the welcoming committee.

Come fall of that year, the black-haired beauty slipped on a new dress and headed out to the Orlando train station. When Fred disembarked from the train, the strangers locked eyes and felt an inexplicable connection, one that transcended mere attraction. "I must say, we were just good friends [at first]," Sara later recalled. "We didn't do much dating, as such. We all had ran around in a group...But I think we thoroughly enjoyed each other's company...and he was a marvelous dancer, a fabulous dancer! So I would ask him to our sorority dances, and he would ask me to his fraternity dances."

In time, the romantic feelings for Fred persisted, and continuously deepened. Fred was always perfectly groomed, and while not bothered by trends, he always appeared dapper. Fred and Sara, both excellent pianists, shared the same sense of humor, and they experienced chemistry like no other when they made music together. In fact, it was not only his kindness and his magnanimity, but his affinity for the piano that weakened Sara's knees in the first place. "He sat right down and started playing some pop stuff," said Sara. "We were so impressed, because none of us could do that...we couldn't just sit down and play jazz...He could do it all..."

Much to Sara's relief, her feelings for Fred were reciprocated. Sara was sharp-witted and immensely gifted, and she was described by her friends as a "firecracker" who illuminated the dullest of rooms with her easygoing presence. To top it all off, the fetching young woman cared deeply about the welfare of all children. The pair continued to enjoy their close friendship, speaking little of their romantic feelings for each other until their ambitions after college drove them apart. After graduating from Rollins, Sara relocated to Tallahassee and resumed her education at Florida State, training with the illustrious Hungarian-American composer, Ernst von Dohnanyi. Meanwhile, following Fred's graduation in 1951, wherein he was honored *magna cum laude*, he hopped on a plane to New York and landed himself an apprenticeship at the National Broadcasting Company (NBC). The two were now separated by over 1,000 miles, and while they immersed themselves in their new environments, their feelings for one another remained unchanged.

Unable to forget one another, the pair exchanged a series of letters over the following months, and as Sara described them, the letters were "mundane," so much so that she eventually lost track of Fred's letters – all but one. One day, completely out of the blue, Sara received a letter with these 4 world-shaking closing words: "Will you marry me?" She dropped all she was doing at once, hastened to the nearest phone booth, and dialed Fred's number. As soon as Fred answered,

Sara blurted "Yes," to which her overjoyed fiancé teasingly replied, "Yes to what? I have no remembrance of it. None at all!" Not long after, Sara wrapped up her studies at Florida State, packed her belongings, and uprooted to the Big Apple. The young couple exchanged their vows in a modest Christian ceremony at a local church on the 9th of June, 1952. They soon had two children, John Frederick and James Byrd.

Fred was constantly swamped with work, but the natural-born family man made a concerted effort to spend what limited free time he had with his wife and children. "Fred was my best friend," a glowing Sara once gushed. "The boys loved him – he was more patient with them than I was!" Those who knew them spoke almost enviously about the Rogers' seemingly picture-perfect marriage. In reality, the pair occasionally bickered and weathered rough patches, just like any other couple, but an audio recording captured from behind the curtains on Fred's set reveals a telling facet to the secret of their healthy relationship. "Sometimes, when we disagree, I feel frustrated," came the muffled voice of Fred, just minutes after a brief spat. "But I never forget how lucky I am to have you [Sara] in my family. Always remember how special you are."

As dissimilar as their personalities were, their compatible beliefs, principles, and dreams further cemented their unbreakable bond. For starters, Mr. and Mrs. Rogers valued the privacy of their children and were so adept at keeping them out of the spotlight that their children, now approaching their 60s, have yet to give a major interview.

In fact, what little is known about the personal lives of the discreet couple is derived from the accounts of family friends, as well as presumptions gathered by the tidbits of information disclosed by Sara herself. "They're very down-to-earth people," said Gloria Cook, a former faculty member of the Rollins Music Department. "They don't like fancy. Even when they come to visit, I don't especially clean the house or put flowers out or the best china. I know that's not them."

The newlyweds had more than an ample amount of cash stashed away in their savings accounts, but the pious couple, rounded by simple tastes, lived frugally. Rarely did they opt for brand products at the grocery store or indulge in sumptuous feasts at upscale restaurants. They purchased almost exclusively secondhand, from their clothes to their furniture, and even their cars.

The famously methodical Fred had something of an obsession with routine. Once he returned home from a grueling day's work, he ate supper and spent a bit of quality time with the kids. After dinner – or following his arrival after an extra-long shift – he washed up, marched up to the master room, settled under the covers, and was out within minutes. The most adventurous part of Fred's daily routine was his habit of swimming laps at the crack of dawn.

At one point, shortly before Fred's graduation from Rollins, he pondered the addition of a theological diploma to his spangling résumé. The God-fearing Fred might have very well followed through with this had it not been for the lowbrow comedy sketch he stumbled upon one fateful afternoon, just days before the end of spring break in 1951. The sketch, part of an unnamed children's program, featured rowdy instrumentals, vulgar slapstick elements, and a patronizing segment that featured nothing but two clowns hurling cream pies at one another. A bewildered Fred soon awoke from his trance and changed the channel, but the shoddy selection of children's shows that were then circulating on national television gnawed at him, and eventually he determined that something had to be done to revolutionize the medium of television, which he deemed was falling pitifully short of its maximum potential. "I got into television because I hated it so," Fred later told CNN. "The television, and soon, the computer, are things like refrigerators. Parents bring them into their homes and present them to their families, and unless they tell them otherwise, kids think the things on television are part of the family tradition. But people wouldn't ordinarily put things in their refrigerators that are detrimental to their health, and they shouldn't let it happen with television."

There were no shortcuts to lasting success in Hollywood, a stark reality that Fred accepted without complaint, but his willingness to work his way up from the lowest tier of the totem pole did little to smooth the rocky course that awaited him. He started out in NBC as a glorified errand boy, tasked with completing coffee runs, note-taking, and other menial duties. He kept to his assignments meticulously, but he remained overlooked and nameless to most of his contemporaries. His superiors only seemed to heed his presence when he messed up, and he later cited the time one of the senior executives berated him in front of his peers after he failed to sprinkle sweetener in the man's coffee.

Nevertheless, Fred persevered. Channeling the patience and resolve of his grandfather, Fred continued to punch in well before he was expected, and he completed his assignments as told, with an exuberant smile on his face all the while. In time, he impressed his superiors enough to be promoted to assistant producer for the following half-hour variety shows (mostly televised spin-offs of established radio programs): *The Kate Smith Hour, Your Lucky Strike Hit Parade, The Voice of Firestone,* and *NBC Opera Theater*. He was also appointed floor director of the Western "general purpose" series, *The Gabby Hayes Show*, which premiered in 1950. Fred was especially taken by the unorthodox production style of the quirky, 15-minute program, more specifically the way the characters often broke the fourth wall and spoke directly to the camera.

Fred remained a faithful employee of NBC until tensions between him and the executives, resulting from the network's refusal to enhance the paltry budget of educational television, boiled over in 1953. To the astonishment of his colleagues, Fred tendered his resignation and announced his intentions to start fresh at *WQED*, a nascent "community-sponsored public television station" based in Pittsburgh. When asked about the motives behind his head-scratching decision, Fred replied, "The people at NBC [told me], 'You're out of your mind! That place isn't even on the air yet!' And I said, 'Well, something tells me that's what I'm supposed to do.' And that was it."

At first, the then-inexperienced Fred resisted the idea of diving into children's programming, but when it was revealed to him that there remained no other vacant positions for him in the network, he tentatively agreed to take a swing at it. As it turned out, he was tapping right into his forte, and in less than a year, Fred – struck by the idea of incorporating his love of puppetry into an educational children's program – partnered with masterly actor and musician Josie Carey to fill the hour-long slot available to them. The show, which they dubbed *The Children's Corner*, made its debut in April of 1954. Though the crew, headed by the dynamic duo – program director Fred and host Josie – was made to operate on a miserly budget, the resourceful Fred was undaunted by the ensuing setbacks. He took this as an opportunity instead to show his audience the wonders of their boundless imaginations. Similarly, the unsophisticated backdrops and adorable, but patently handcrafted puppets pushed children watching to create their own felt friends and miniature puppet theaters, thereby exercising their creativity and sharpening their skills of independence.

Throughout his stint on the *The Children's Corner*, Fred elected to remain off-camera. Apart from the numerous responsibilities attached to the title of program director, Fred worked with Josie to design the characters and to flesh out the show's concepts, storylines, and original musical numbers. The show was initially green-lit as a quarter-hour "filler" inserted between cartoons and "daily...educational films for children," but not long after the zealous campaigns of Fred and Josie, the network agreed to bump them up to the hour-long slot. Only then did they unveil an assortment of marionette characters for the first time, such as "Daniel Striped Tiger," "King Friday XIII," "X the Owl," "Henrietta," and the deliciously bizarre socialite "Lady Elaine Fairchilde" (supposedly named after his sister), most of which were shifted to his later show.

It was the bubbly personality and honeyed voice of the 24-year-old Josie that drew in the young crowd. Far more than a pretty face, the multi-talented Josie was an integral component of the *Corner's* high ratings. Like Fred, Josie started out as a lowly secretary to Dorothy Daniels, the first manager of the *WQED*. Determined to break out of the mold the network had confined her in, she struggled doubly hard to make a name for herself, and Josie finally landed on her superiors' radar when she took the initiative to knock on every door she came across, luring potential viewers in with *WQED* programs and even procuring $2 donations for the fledgling network.

Fred worked well with Josie because he made up for the traits and skills Josie lacked, and vice versa. They spent the bulk of their time in front of a piano, with Fred testing out new melodies and Josie completing them with catchy lyrics. Not only did the partners churn out 68 songs together, they co-wrote and co-directed almost all of the episodes of the show. Said Josie about their very first show, "That was the longest hour that I can remember. We had it planned out pretty well. It was probably the best children's program anybody [had] ever done because it had something for everybody, and we were aiming at the 8 to 12-year-olds. So we had a club and we stole from the Boy Scouts and the Girl Scouts...we got their handbooks and found out what it was that made a good club...and used some of those rules. [And] we had our own songs."

Fred was endlessly reflective – at times, to a fault – but his objectives, insisted Josie, had been selfless from the very beginning. "Fred does Fred. And Fred is Fred," said Josie. "He's very aware of what should be said to small children. I think he has to be credited with that because there were many times we were asked to do things or could have done things that were perhaps financially good, but Fred said 'no.' Because all along, he wanted to do a program. Even in the early days, it was never a show, always a program..."

Fred's wife, Sara, was another crucial cog for the show's success and the upward trajectory of her husband's career. For one, she was a regular extra who voiced the inanimate objects and other background characters on the program. She also dedicated at least two hours of her day to filing away and responding to the rambling letters sent to the offices from the series' biggest fan club, the Tame Tigers Torganization. Only after the birth of their second son did Sara withdraw from the industry, but her essence forever remained, immortalized in one of Fred's favorite puppets: Queen Sara Saturday, the most elegant and "gracious puppet" on the small screen.

In 1955, Fred's work was recognized for the first time when *The Children's Corner* was awarded the Sylvania Award – a short-lived distinction that once vied with the Emmy Award in prestige – for excellence in educational programming. The hit series continued to mesmerize the young minds of America until its last season in 1961.

Fred's extracurricular accomplishments during his 7-year tenure as the co-writer, co-producer, and chief puppeteer on *The Children's Corner* – which included the juggling of a master's education in divinity at Pittsburgh Theological Seminary –serves as a testament to his tenacity. He further enriched his curriculum vitae by enrolling in a child psychology course at the Arsenal Family and Children Center in the same city. It was here that Fred met Dr. Margaret McFarland, a venerable child psychologist and the associate professor in the University of Pittsburgh's Department of Psychiatry.

Margaret, who had assisted the center's co-founder, Dr. Benjamin Spock, in assembling the university's child care development program back in 1952, was employed as the resident psychiatrist and consultant of Fred's shows, from *The Children's Corner* and beyond. Her expertise with children, fortified by her comprehensive credentials and refined by her extensive experience with young folk and educators (including the 4 years she spent in Australia training kindergarten teachers) made her an ideal fit for the job. Not only was Margaret well-versed in child developmental theories, she had a knack for understanding the emotional behavior of a wide range of children. Margaret and Fred convened weekly to analyze narratives, song lyrics, scripts, and even the props used in the show.

Fred later claimed that Margaret's exceptional insight rectified prospectively disastrous episodes on more than one occasion. When Fred proposed an episode that revolved around the theme of fire, for example, Margaret quickly shut him down. "She helped me...realize that it was essential to deal with control of fluids before even introducing anything about fire," Fred explained. "I learned, for instance, that most children's dreams about fire center around their control of their own body fluids! That's how personal a 'fire' can seem to a child."

Other advice coming from Margaret left its mark to such a degree that it became a driving commandment behind his work. "[You must] offer the kids who you really are because they'll know what's really important to you." She was among the first to urge him to use his passion for music as a means to connect with his young viewers. "They'll find their own way," said Margaret. "But [you must] show them that there's a way that really means something to you..."

In 1962, a year after the *Corner's* finale, Fred secured his master's diploma in theology and was officially ordained as a minister by the United Presbyterian Church the following year. The Church elders deliberated over the placement of Fred within their community for some time, but after considering all their options, he was charged with serving as a missionary to the children through the medium of television. The initial plan was to roll out a church-produced television program bearing similar, but more Christian-oriented themes to that of *The Children's Corner*. Ultimately, the funding fell through and the project met its demise.

It was then that the Fred Rainsberry, director of Children's Programming for the Canadian Broadcasting Corporation (CBC), swooped in on Fred. Rainsberry invited him to their headquarters in Toronto and offered him a brand new children's program, consisting of 15-minute episodes, complete with marionettes and music. Rainsberry's one condition was for Fred himself to step out from behind the camera, thereby making him the star of his very own show. In the summer of 1962, Fred, Sara, and their infant children moved in to a humble two-story home just a few blocks away from CBC's main office.

By fall of 1963, the new program, entitled *"Misterogers,"* was ready to air its first episode. The program performed splendidly before the children of America's neighbors, and in 1964, the series was renewed and picked up by a network in Pittsburgh. Heeding what was clearly a vehement demand for the show, Eastern Educational Network (EEN), also known as American Public Television (APT), ordered from Fred another 100 episodes.

Following the conclusion of the 100th episode in early 1965, Fred handed in his notice and moved his family back to Pittsburgh. For a few months, he resumed his research on child development and conducted volunteer work with the children of Bellefield Presbyterian as WQED board members appealed to patrons for the financing of another fully-fledged children's program. Making the most out of his "free time," Fred accepted a seasonal project with the WTAE, another local television station, serving as host of a Sunday afternoon program that ran from October to December of 1965.

By the winter of 1966, WQED had finally acquired enough funding to launch Fred's educational program, *Mister Rogers' Neighborhood*. The first season, which aired in the Pittsburgh region between October 1966 and May 1967, enjoyed spectacular ratings. EEN was keen to broadcast the program in select cities – namely, Boston, Miami, San Francisco, New York, and Washington, D.C., – but the network's depleted treasury birthed a dreary cloud of cancellations that loomed over *Mister Rogers' Neighborhood* crew.

In a bid to raise awareness about the program, WGBH in Boston held a last-minute fundraiser for the show. The organizers anxiously prepared for the event, fearing an inability to fill even half of the 500 seats in the facility, but the ensuing turnout blew them clear out of the water as a staggering crowd of over 10,000 showed up to voice their support. Confronted with the indisputable demand of the public, the Sears-Roebuck Foundation agreed to sponsor the production of *Mister Rogers' Neighborhood* from that point forward.

Thus, on the 19th of February, 1968, American children from across the country tuned in to *Mister Rogers' Neighborhood* for the first time. Later that year, Fred was named chairman of the Forum on Mass Media and Child Development of the White House Conference on Youth.

A picture of Rogers on set during the late 1960s

In May of the following year, Fred was summoned to the Senate Hearings on Public Television in Washington, D.C. and invited to testify before the Senate Subcommittee on Communication. Just a few weeks prior, President Richard Nixon issued a proposal that aimed to shrink the budget for public television in half to better fund the controversial Vietnam War. 41-year-old

Fred, due to speak before Rhode Island Senator and committee chairman John Pastore, was intent on changing his mind.

Nixon

Pastore

Dressed in a crisp black suit paired with a navy-blue tie, the thick tuft of hair above his receding hairline tidily slicked back, Fred had an aura of quiet confidence about him. He reeled in those around him not with flashy terms, but plain words packed with a heartfelt punch: "This is what I give. I give an expression of care every day to each child, to help him realize that he is unique. I end the program by saying, 'You've made this day a special day, by just your being you. There's no person in the whole world like you, and I like you, just the way you are'...I feel that if we in public television can...make it clear that feelings are mentionable and manageable, we will have done a great service for mental health..."

Fred ended his speech by reading aloud the lyrics to one of his songs: "What do you do with the mad that you feel? When you feel so mad you could bite? When the whole wide world seems oh so wrong...Do you punch a bag? Do you pound some clay or some dough? Do you round up friends for a game of tag or see how fast you go? It's great to be able to stop when you've planned the thing that's wrong. And be able to do something else instead – and think this song..."

Senator Pastore had never seen the program, nor had he ever met the man behind it prior to this day, but his eyes were touched by a faint glisten. "I'm supposed to be a pretty tough guy," said Pastore. "[But] this is the first time I've had goosebumps for the last 2 days. Looks like you just earned the $20 million." In under 6 minutes, Fred had convinced Pastore to more than double the funding for public television.

Mister Rogers' Neighborhood

"I feel that those of us in television are chosen to be servants. It doesn't mater what our particular job, we are chosen to help meet the deeper needs of those who watch and listen – day and night." – attributed to Fred Rogers

In 1971, Fred established *Family Communications, Inc.,* also known as the *"Fred Rogers Company,"* a non-profit organization and production company that vowed to bring wholesome, educational, and "family-oriented" content to children across the continent.

All the while, *Mister Rogers' Neighborhood* was far more than just a stable source of income; it was an unprecedented platform that allowed him to touch upon hard-hitting subject matters, not by diluting them with superficial or schematic euphemisms but by carefully deconstructing them or weaving serious topics into the storylines. Fred treated his guests, children and grown-up alike with fatherly warmth and sincerity, but it was the respect he showed towards his "neighbors," no matter their age, color, or size, that resonated with his young viewers. Fred explained to CNN in the early 2000s, "The whole idea is to look at the television camera and present as much love as you possibly could to a person who might feel that he or she needs it...The world is not always a kind place. That's something all children learn for themselves, whether we want them to or not, but it's something they really need our help to understand." David Kleeman, Executive Director of the American Center for Children and Media in Des Plaines, added the following: "[Fred] made a mass medium personal. He had a way of talking to the camera as though there was just one child there. And he made every child feel he was speaking directly to them."

Many once involved in the production of *Mister Rogers' Neighborhood* have ascribed the program's prosperity to Fred's exquisite attention to detail. Every narrative, designed to exemplify "a neighborhood expression of care," was fastidiously framed with children's psychological interests in mind. Fred was mindful of his paternal role, and he sought to educate the masses about proper manners, good conduct, and upstanding moral values through tasteful puppetry and song. He chose insentient objects – mostly puppets – and animated them with colorful voices during skits. Children were often on *Mister Rogers' Neighborhood*, and when they were, Fred often opted against featuring more than one child, hoping to stave off any subconscious feelings of sibling rivalry. Even Fred's tennis shoes served a dual purpose - apart from their homely quality, they were conveniently quiet, allowing him to move around and sneak backstage to direct the puppets soundlessly.

Interestingly enough, while Fred himself was a devoted Christian and a proud patriot, he was not one to force his beliefs and customs upon others, so he almost never included religious topics. He did not want to alienate children of other faiths or cultures, instead focusing on universal values and promoting life lessons that applied to all.

His attention to detail extended to the wardrobe, set design, and general aesthetics of *Mister Rogers' Neighborhood.* The stoplight's blinking yellow light, seen in the first shot of the title sequence, is a subliminal reminder, directed towards both parent and child, to settle down, for it was time for the program. Hedda Sharapan, Director of Early Childhood Initiatives at *The Fred Rogers Company*, expounded the reasoning behind the choreography: "[Fred] changed to his sweater, sang the same welcoming song, and sat on the bench to change his sneakers. This predictability offered a sense of security. Through your rituals and routines, you're offering that to children, too."

Familiarity, comfort, and gentle authority were foundational elements of Fred's relationship with his young audience. He presented himself as an adult, and he never resorted to garish gags or hackneyed costumes to capture the attention of his viewers, for he firmly believed they were capable of consuming far more depth. Instead, he donned a single-color cardigan, slacks, canvas tennis shoes, and a traditional haircut, relying on substance as opposed to glamour. At the same time, while he aimed to underscore a certain dominance that would command obedience, his switching to a comfortable cardigan and tennis shoes, as well as the benign tone of his voice, was meant to keep the children at ease. It was important to Fred that the children viewed him as not only a teacher, but also a friend they could trust.

The casual, yet intimate atmosphere provided by Fred's sets – from *The Children's Corner* to *Mister Rogers' Neighborhood* – allowed him to better broach uncomfortable, but critical facts of life, such as death, divorce, disabilities, and so on. Fred also chose to tackle current events, both laudable and deplorable, such as the assassination of Senator Robert Kennedy, in the hopes of helping children better understand these sensitive issues.

The unusually diverse community within *Mister Rogers' Neighborhood* was designed to accustom his audience to the rainbow of races, cultures, and lifestyles often neglected in the media. The program also provided Fred with the opportunity to voice his stance regarding contentious issues during the time.

The year the program premiered nationwide in 1968, racial tensions were at their peak, aggravated by the assassination of Martin Luther King, Jr., in early April. Throngs of the fallen Dr. King's infuriated supporters rioted, lashing out at the authorities and looting the properties of civilians. This triggered a new wave of what historians termed "white flight," or the mass migration of white citizens to "racially homogeneous" or white-majority neighborhoods. Fred's decision to feature Mrs. Saunders, an African-American teacher, along with a small class of interracial students, was no coincidence, and the casting of African-American characters was not a one-off occurrence. Those who accused the producers of inauthenticity and milking "trends," were proved wrong when he introduced Officer Clemmons, the neighborhood policeman, in August 1968. Not only were audiences presented with the "startling image" of an African-

American man in uniform, marking him as a figure of authority and security, Officer Clemmons became the first recurring African-American character on a children's program.

Fred took his agenda one step further with an episode in 1969 in which he takes a plastic kiddie pool out into the yard and fills it to the brim with water from a hose. When Fred spots Officer Clemmons around the corner, he promptly invites him in for a seat, and to soak his feet in the pool. The image was simple enough, but the symbolism of a black man and white man sharing a quick dip in the pool at a time when almost all facilities were segregated carried with it an impactful message. Tying it all together was a seemingly trivial, but moving gesture. Clemmons explained, "The icon Fred Rogers not only was showing my brown skin in the tub with his white skin as 2 friends, but as I was getting out of that tub, he was helping me dry my feet."

Fred also made it a point to feature strong female characters with respectable careers typically reserved for men in that day and age. In one 1975 episode, aired two years after Compton Mayor Doris A. Davis made history as the first female African-American mayor, Fred paid tribute by introducing Mayor Maggie – played by African-American actress Maggie Stewart – to the show. Mayor Maggie of Westwood was more than the diversity cast the jaded have branded her to be; she was an intellectual, independent, and self-made woman who served as King Friday XIII's equal. Additionally, the sidekick Mayor Maggie was paired with, Associate Mayor Aber (played by the sandy-haired and alabaster Chuck Aber), provided the audience with yet another fresh dynamic.

Fred's ability to reserve judgment despite his faith was another contributor to the show's longevity. Not only was he able to assemble a cast and crew composed of premium talent, the team was a family. Though misunderstandings, disagreements, and clashing beliefs were not uncommon, brotherly loyalty and neighborly love bound them as one.

However, some of Fred's Christian peers and his conservative viewers found his acceptance excessive and sycophantic. His employment of LGBT crew and staff, such as François Clemmons and the operatic John Reardon from *Mister Rogers' Neighborhood* of Make-Believe, and his close friendship with them outside of the show, turned off a fraction of narrow-minded viewers and others aware of the fact. The most bitter went so far as to accuse Fred of being a "false Christian," chastising him for his association with homosexual crew members and patronage at the 6th Presbyterian Church in Pittsburgh, one of the region's few LGBT-friendly churches.

"The significance of Fred [hiring] a black gay man is not lost," Clemmons later shared. "I felt unworthy, like Peter in the Bible. Why did he choose me?" As tolerant of the LGBT community as Fred was, there was not a single character who identified as such in all 31 seasons of the show. Gay cast and crew members were also instructed by Fred to remain in the closet for some time. Fred once said to Clemmons, "Franc, we've come to love you here in *Mister Rogers' Neighborhood.* You have talents and gifts that set you apart and above the crowd, and we want to ensure your place with us...Now I want you to know, Franc, that if you're gay, it doesn't matter to me at all. Whatever you say and do is fine with me, but if you're going to be on the show...you can't be 'out'...People must not know...Many of the wrong people will get the worst idea, and we don't want them thinking and talking about you like that. If those people put up enough fuss, then I couldn't have you on the program. It's not an issue for me. I don't think you're less of a person. I don't think you're immoral."

While Fred had no intention of expelling Clemmons or Reardon from production, he reportedly advised his staff to find a woman to settle down with, advice that the former took. It was only when Clemmons' marriage inevitably failed that Fred witnessed his devastation, extended an earnest apology, and retracted his statements. Fred eventually encouraged Clemmons to feel free to express his sexuality, guarded him from prejudice and bigotry, and urged him to find a companion who would truly make him happy.

During the filming of Officer Clemmons' last appearance in 1993, Fred concluded the episode with his trademark final words: "You make every day a special day just by being you, and I like you just the way you are." But this time, he was looking off-camera, straight into Clemmons' misty eyes. After the show, Clemmons asked him, "Fred, were you talking to me?" Fred replied, "Yes. I have been talking to you for years. But you heard me today."

As is the case with most film and television productions, the actual making of *Mister Rogers' Neighborhood* was not without its share of stresses and problems, ranging from mild to chaotic. It comes as little surprise that a show with such depth and attention to detail was spearheaded by a perfectionist, and Fred functioned at his best when adhering to a routine. When on set, he disliked almost every form of spontaneity, from ad-libbing and improvisation to unexpected setbacks. He much preferred to stick to the script as is, and he exerted great effort in executing the choreography and landing on all markers to a tee.

Fred's obsession with bringing as much realism – puppets and Neighborhood of Make-Believe aside – as he could into the program occasionally led to creative disagreements. When he invited a marine biologist, Sylvia Earle, to his show, he fitted his aquarium with a microphone to demonstrate to the audience the sounds that fish make when they eat. The filming ostensibly screeched to a halt when the fish refused to eat, but rather than cry "cut," Fred hovered in the background quietly. The crew later offered to film the segment again, but Fred, who took it as an opportunity to teach his viewers about the value of patience, declined.

Joe Negri, better known as "Handyman Negri" from *Mister Rogers' Neighborhood,* said this about his employer: "[Fred] was very demanding in his gentle way. He wrote the scripts, and he wanted them done exactly as he wrote them...He wanted to be an advocate for kids, and he hated commercials. He wanted to be on public broadcasting, because he didn't want to have a show that companies could use to sell products."

A few of the crewmen sought to relieve their stresses by poking fun at the man in charge. They often mocked Fred's old-fangled wardrobe and timid mannerisms, and they ridiculed his straight-laced principles behind his back. Even so, it was Fred whom many privately approached when bogged down by their personal problems. Fred, who never turned a "neighbor" in need away, was an extraordinary listener, and he provided them with advice regarding their rocky marriages, troubled children, financial difficulties, and so forth, at times through his beloved puppets.

The formula he devised – made up of equal parts creativity, music, life lessons, and educational value – was innovative in more ways than one. It wasn't just the simplicity and success of the show that stumped numerous experts, but also the show's scientific merits. A Yale study that juxtaposed *Mister Rogers' Neighborhood* with *Sesame Street* discovered that children who watched the former remembered the narratives and moral lessons longer. Children who watched *Mister Rogers' Neighborhood* were also more likely to display higher "tolerances of delay," which meant that their patience for attention and treats exceeded that of the latter group. Similarly, a 1969 issue from *The Atlantic* published an independent study on the dialogue used in the program. They found that Fred's audience was exceptionally susceptible to "byplay," a phenomenon wherein children vocally respond to questions and interactive statements posed to them by Rogers.

The relationships some children formed with the TV personality are even more deep-seated. A 1998 edition of *Esquire* tells the story of one such viewer, a young boy diagnosed with "an acute case of autism." Those around him, including his parents, assumed he was mute, but one day he pointed at one of Fred's puppets on the television screen and stated matter-of-factly, "X the Owl." What's more, the boy, who never made eye contact with either of his parents, broke the pattern indefinitely when his father invited him to *Mister Rogers' Neighborhood* of Make-Believe. From that day onward, the boy not only began to speak regularly, he learned how to read, a turnaround so dramatic that it galvanized his father to seek out Fred so that he could express his gratitude in person.

On August 31, 2001, after 31 seasons, 865 episodes, and the production of over 200 original songs, America's favorite neighbor hung up his coat, slipped on his sweater and sneakers, and welcomed his children home for the last time.

Goodbye, Neighbor

"I'm convinced that when we help our children find healthy ways of dealing with their feelings – ways that don't hurt them or anyone else – we're helping to make our world a safer, better place." – attributed to Fred Rogers

Fred Rogers might be most recognizable as the nostalgic face of America's childhood, but his influence stretched beyond television.

As 1975 began to draw to a close, Sony unleashed the videocassette recorder, or the "VCR," on the American market. The nation was abuzz with excitement, and for good reason, as such a thing was radically new. 1975 was a time when television owners had to actually get up to change the channels.

While the masses marveled over and pined after the futuristic contraption, film corporations and television studios were positively livid. Just months later, in a desperate attempt to freeze the production and distribution of the Betamax, Walt Disney Productions and Universal Studios simultaneously filed lawsuits against Sony. The sale of the Betamax, which, the corporate lawyers asserted, would only breed unauthorized distribution and flagrant copyright infringement, was as unjust as it was unlawful, for it would almost certainly cost the studios millions of dollars in lost revenue.

In 1983, the high-profile case *Universal Studios v. Sony Corporation of America* reached the Supreme Court. The former party was more disconcerted than they had ever been, for at this stage, close to half of all American households were VCR owners. Likewise, videocassettes were threatening to give traditional box office sales a run for their money.

Rogers, a proponent of educational materials as public domain and the responsible utilization of media, was invited to testify on behalf of *Sony*. He said, "I have always felt that with the advent of all of this new technology that allows people to tape *Mister Rogers' Neighborhood* off-the-air...they then become much more active in the programming of their family's television life. Very frankly, I am opposed to people being programmed by others. My whole approach in broadcasting has always been 'You are an important person just the way you are. You can make healthy decisions'...I just feel that anything that allows a person to be more active in the control of his or her life, in a healthy way, is important."

The Supreme Court ultimately sided with *Sony*, a democratic victory evidently molded by Fred's comments, for he was quoted in the final ruling: "[Fred] testified that he had absolutely no objection to home taping for noncommercial use and expressed the opinion that it is a real service to families to be able to record children's programs and to show them at appropriate times."

Fred remained active throughout his short retirement. He continued to busy himself with charity work and his still-thriving book business – despite being so immersed in his television show, he also authored 35 books for children, parents, and aspiring child psychologists. Moreover, he produced a number of documentaries, such as *Mister Rogers' Heroes* and *Old Friends, New Friends*, to name a few. He returned to the public eye sporadically with appearances on late night talk shows, a special with Koko the Gorilla, and he even tried his hand at acting with his guest role in the CBS American Western drama, *Dr. Quinn, Medicine Woman.*

It's doubtful a trophy cabinet would have been big enough to store the collection of awards he received during his career. On top of 40 honorary degrees, Fred was the recipient of 4 daytime Emmys, a 1997 Lifetime Achievement award from the National Academy of Television Arts and Sciences, and the Presidential Medal of Freedom in 2002, presented to him and the now-disgraced Bill Cosby by President George W. Bush.

Rogers meeting with President Bush

Naturally, the internet has given rise to scores of urban legends, from riveting theories to downright bizarre accusations. One such legend accuses Fred of concealing a ghastly, violent past. According to this legend, he was once a merciless Navy Seal, or perhaps a sniper, with a vicious thirst for blood and an ominous record of over 150 kills during the Vietnam War. Others have stamped Fred as a fully-inked, escaped convict turned professional con artist. According to them, Fred supposedly insisted upon wearing those cardigans to hide the offensive tattoos under his sleeves, and this, they say, is why one will never find a photograph of Fred Rogers in a short-sleeved shirt. As riveting as these rumors may be, they are simply fascinating fabrications that can be discredited with a simple search online.

In the same vein, there are a few who genuinely take offense to Fred's principles. Don Chance, a professor of finance from the Louisiana State University, is one of Fred's fiercest critics. Chance has, on more than one occasion, denigrated Fred's character as a sham, and he believes Rogers' legacy is a joke that is largely responsible for producing lazy, whiny millennials and "a culture of excessive doting."

It seems any attempt to figure out what kind of man Fred Rogers really was depends on the source. Many journalists flagged him down for interviews following his retirement, and they would find themselves at a loss for words. Fred reportedly had a habit of turning the tables around, distracting journalists with questions of his own and snapping multiple photographs of them. Fred then compiled the pictures into a photo album and mailed it to the journalists. The gentleman was also equipped with a phenomenal memory; he occasionally rang up the journalist for a quick chat, asking questions about their family members and important events in their lives, and apparently never forgetting a single detail.

Notwithstanding the whirlwind of touching tales about Fred Rogers that continue to emerge to this day, he still had flaws and obvious eccentricities. Fred made it a point to answer every single piece of fan mail directed to him, spending hours on end coming up with customized responses. He took to heart the words of everyone who reached out to him, for they not only showered him with the usual kudos and praises, but confided in him during their darkest hours. And though Fred was not one to hold grudges or lose his temper, he was a rather nervous man who could get frustrated easily. Whenever he felt overwhelmed, he turned to the piano, and pacified himself with a calming melody. On set, he was also known to mutter "mercy" repetitively under his breath whenever things failed to go as planned, even at times letting slip an actual curse word or two. Rogers also had a strange fixation with his weight - he climbed onto his bathroom scale each morning to make sure that his weight remained at exactly 143 pounds (65 kilograms), the traditional code for "I love you."

A year after Fred's retirement, he was diagnosed with stomach cancer, and though he was operated on, his health continued to deteriorate until he passed away peacefully, surrounded by his loved ones, on February 27, 2003.

To say that the world lost one of its brightest stars would be an understatement. That said, millions of children around the world can find solace in the following words, taken from one of his last known recordings with WQED: "I would like to tell you what I often told you when you were much younger. I like you just the way you are. And what's more, I'm so grateful to you for helping the children in your life to know that you'll do everything you can to keep them safe. And to help them express their feelings in ways that will bring healing in many different neighborhoods...It's such a good feeling to know that we're lifelong friends."

Lee Paxton's picture of a statue of Rogers in Pittsburgh

Online Resources

Other titles about Mister Rogers on Amazon

Bibliography

Editors, B. *Fred Rogers Biography*. 30 Jan. 2018, www.biography.com/people/fred-rogers-9462161. Accessed 2 Apr. 2018.

Editors, S. *Mr. Rogers' Rumor Neighborhood*. 29 June 2007, www.snopes.com/fact-check/fred-rogers-rumors/. Accessed 2 Apr. 2018.

Emery, D. *Was Mr. Rogers a Navy SEAL or Marine Sniper?* 3 Nov. 2017, www.thoughtco.com/was-mr-rogers-a-navy-seal-or-marine-sniper-3299333. Accessed 2 Apr. 2018.

Blakemore, E. *Why Are There So Many Urban Legends About Mr. Rogers?* 16 Feb. 2018, www.history.com/news/urban-legends-mr-rogers. Accessed 2 Apr. 2018.

English, J. *35 Things You Might Not Know About Mister Rogers*. 20 July 2017, mentalfloss.com/article/49561/35-things-you-might-not-know-about-mister-rogers. Accessed 2 Apr. 2018.

Editors, M F. *15 Heartwarming Facts About Mister Rogers*. 20 Mar. 2018, mentalfloss.com/article/93430/15-heartwarming-facts-about-mister-rogers. Accessed 2 Apr. 2018.

Hattikudur, M. *15 Reasons Mister Rogers Was The Best Neighbor Ever*. 23 May 2007, mentalfloss.com/article/16416/15-reasons-mister-rogers-was-best-neighbor-ever. Accessed 2 Apr. 2018.

Keeley, M. *Understanding the Quiet Gay Activism of Mister Rogers*. 25 Dec. 2017, hornet.com/stories/mister-rogers-gay-activism-quiet/. Accessed 2 Apr. 2018.

Stewart, S. *Mr. Rogers Really Was the Nicest Guy Ever*. 23 Jan. 2018, nypost.com/2018/01/23/mr-rogers-really-was-the-nicest-guy-ever/. Accessed 2 Apr. 2018.

Varnum, K. *Behind the Scenes in Mr. Rogers' Neighborhood* . 17 Aug. 2003, www.authorsden.com/visit/viewshortstory.asp?id=9402. Accessed 2 Apr. 2018.

Editors, T T. *Heartwarming / Mister Rogers' Neighborhood*. 2018, tvtropes.org/pmwiki/pmwiki.php/Heartwarming/MisterRogersNeighborhood. Accessed 2 Apr. 2018.

Editors, I. *A Mr Rogers Story (in Description)*. 3 Sept. 2014, imgur.com/gallery/hhWJUSp. Accessed 2 Apr. 2018.

Editors, A L. *Mr. Rogers Invited the Limo Driver into the House and Sat up Front*. 16 May 2013, www.alearned.com/limo-driver/. Accessed 2 Apr. 2018.

Editors, S. *Remorseful Car Thieves*. June 2003, www.snopes.com/fact-check/remorseful-car-thieves/. Accessed 2 Apr. 2018.

Claxton, Z. *Mr. Rogers*. 6 Jan. 2010, zakclaxton.blogspot.tw/2010/01/mr-rogers.html. Accessed 2 Apr. 2018.

Zambelli, A. *18 Things You Didn't Know About Mister Rogers*. 14 Nov. 2015, www.goodhousekeeping.com/life/entertainment/g2940/mister-rogers-facts/. Accessed 2 Apr. 2018.

Editors, F. *40 Neighborly Facts about Mr. Rogers.* 22 Mar. 2018, www.factinate.com/people/40-facts-neighborly-facts-about-mr-rogers/. Accessed 2 Apr. 2018.

Editors, E. *Fred McFeely Rogers*. 2004, www.encyclopedia.com/people/literature-and-arts/film-and-television-biographies/fred-mcfeely-rogers. Accessed 2 Apr. 2018.

Rowles, D. *A Comforting Face In Difficult Times: 20 Things You Might Not Know About Mr. Rogers*. 16 Apr. 2013, uproxx.com/tv/a-comforting-face-in-times-of-tragedy-20-things-you-might-not-know-about-mr-rogers/. Accessed 2 Apr. 2018.

Carpenter, W. *What You Don't Know About Mister Rogers*. 22 Mar. 2012, www.yahoo.com/news/blogs/upshot/don-t-know-mister-rogers-003202984.html. Accessed 2 Apr. 2018.

Editors, V S. *Fred Rogers (1928 - 2003)*. 30 Oct. 2008, www.vancouversun.com/touch/fred rogers 1928 2003/919934/story.html. Accessed 2 Apr. 2018.

Long, M G. *Was Mister Rogers Racist? Twelve Facts About Our Favorite Neighbor*. 7 Aug. 2015, www.huffingtonpost.com/michael-g-long/was-mister-rogers-racist-_b_7939498.html. Accessed 2 Apr. 2018.

Editors, N A. *Episode 1160*. 2008, www.neighborhoodarchive.com/mrn/episodes/1160/index.html. Accessed 3 Apr. 2018.

Carter, A. *This Mr. Rogers Story Will Probably Make You Cry*. 23 May 2017, www.usatoday.com/story/news/nation-now/2017/05/23/mr-rogers-story-probably-make-you-cry/340111001/. Accessed 3 Apr. 2018.

Woo, E. *From the Archives: It's a Sad Day in This Neighborhood*. 28 Feb. 2003, www.latimes.com/local/obituaries/la-me-fred-rogers-20030228-story.html. Accessed 3 Apr. 2018.

Hendrickson, P. *In the Land of Make Believe, The Real Mister Rogers*. 18 Nov. 1982, www.washingtonpost.com/archive/lifestyle/1982/11/18/in-the-land-of-make-believe-the-real-mister-rogers/7ca0e14f-5f91-48e0-932c-898e24970890/?utm_term=.448550d35194. Accessed 3 Apr. 2018.

Editors, R C. *GROWING UP IN LATROBE*. 2015, www.fredrogerscenter.org/about-us/about-fred/early-life/. Accessed 3 Apr. 2018.

Wagner, B. *46 Things I Learned Making Mister Rogers & Me*. 2016, mentalfloss.com/article/49559/46-things-i-learned-making-mister-rogers-me. Accessed 3 Apr. 2018.

Hohenadel, K. *Please Won't You Be My Inspiration?* 16 Mar. 2012, www.nytimes.com/2012/03/18/arts/television/mr-rogers-me-recalls-mr-rogers-neighborhood-on-pbs.html. Accessed 3 Apr. 2018.

Rivero, L. *Mister Rogers' Emotional Neighborhood.* 21 Mar. 2012, www.psychologytoday.com/us/blog/creative-synthesis/201203/mister-rogers-emotional-neighborhood. Accessed 3 Apr. 2018.

Whitbourne, K. *5 Things You Didn't Know About Mister Rogers.* 20 Mar. 2017, entertainment.howstuffworks.com/5-things-you-didnt-know-mister-rogers.htm. Accessed 3 Apr. 2018.

Madigan, T. *: "I'm Proud of You": My Friendship With Fred Rogers.* 11 Aug. 2016, www.unheralded.fish/tag/im-proud-of-you-my-friendship-with-fred-rogers/. Accessed 3 Apr. 2018.

Editors, N A. *The Latrobean.* 2015, www.neighborhoodarchive.com/merch/other/yearbooks/index.html. Accessed 3 Apr. 2018.

Myers, E K. *Remembering Fred Rogers.* 2009, www.lvwonline.org/downloads/LR2009/2proof16470_INSIDELoyalhannaReview.pdf. Accessed 3 Apr. 2018.

Marks, G. *Mr. Rogers' Words Of Kindness Are Still Important Today.* 6 June 2017, www.huffingtonpost.com/entry/mr-rogers-words-of-kindness-are-still-important-today_us_5936afc2e4b0cca4f42d9d56. Accessed 3 Apr. 2018.

Wenham, K. *Mother Teresa's Sainthood Is a Fraud, Just Like She Was.* 7 Sept. 2016, medium.com/@KittyWenham/mother-teresas-sainthood-is-a-fraud-just-like-she-was-eb395177572. Accessed 3 Apr. 2018.

Connellan, M. *Women Suffer from Gandhi's Legacy.* 27 Jan. 2010, www.theguardian.com/commentisfree/2010/jan/27/mohandas-gandhi-women-india. Accessed 3 Apr. 2018.

Editors, A C. *THE EVIL SIDE OF GANDHI ..* 20 Jan. 2013, www.ashtarcommandcrew.net/forum/topics/the-evil-side-of-gandhi. Accessed 3 Apr. 2018.

Gallagher, B. *The 25 Most Offensive Moments in Fox News History.* 12 Sept. 2013, www.complex.com/pop-culture/2013/09/most-offensive-fox-news-moments/fox-friends-call-mr-rogers-evil-evil-man. Accessed 4 Apr. 2018.

Montanez, V. *Now the Crazies Are Coming for Mister Rogers*. 26 Aug. 2013, www.pittsburghmagazine.com/Pittsburgh-Magazine/September-2013/Now-the-Crazies-are-Coming-for-Mister-Rogers/. Accessed 4 Apr. 2018.

Barish, K. *Mr. Rogers, Evil? Really?* 7 Sept. 2013, www.huffingtonpost.com/kenneth-barish-phd/mr-rogers-evil-really_b_3549891.html. Accessed 4 Apr. 2018.

Hattikudur, M. *15 Reasons Mr. Rogers Was Best Neighbor Ever*. 28 July 2008, edition.cnn.com/2008/LIVING/wayoflife/07/28/mf.mrrogers.neighbor/. Accessed 4 Apr. 2018.

Editors, F R. *Remembering Fred Rogers*. 2018, www.fredrogers.org/fred-rogers/. Accessed 4 Apr. 2018.

Editors, F R. *Fred Rogers - Biography*. 2018, www.fredrogers.org/fred-rogers/bio/. Accessed 4 Apr. 2018.

Editors, H C. *Lindbergh Baby Kidnapped*. 2012, www.history.com/this-day-in-history/lindbergh-baby-kidnapped. Accessed 4 Apr. 2018.

Editors, G. *Frederick Brooks McFeely*. 22 Feb. 2015, www.geni.com/people/Frederick-McFeely/6000000015884599727. Accessed 4 Apr. 2018.

Strunk, D. *17 Quotes From Mister Rogers The World Really Needs Right Now*. 23 May 2017, www.buzzfeed.com/delaneystrunk/17-mister-roger-quotes-the-world-really-needs-right-now?utm_term=.svg6KwzQv#.bh5yJ3grz. Accessed 4 Apr. 2018.

Kamenetz, A. *Why Mr. Rogers Is Having A Big Moment In Education*. 24 May 2014, www.npr.org/sections/ed/2014/05/24/314286509/why-mr-rogers-is-having-a-big-moment-in-education. Accessed 4 Apr. 2018.

Editors, D M. *Fred Rogers '50 (1928-2003)*. 2013, dartmouthalumnimagazine.com/articles/fred-rogers-'50-1928-2003. Accessed 4 Apr. 2018.

Long, M G. *'Wasn't He Gay?': A Revealing Question About Mister Rogers*. 2 Feb. 2016, www.huffingtonpost.com/michael-g-long/wasnt-he-gay-a-revealing-_b_6014538.html. Accessed 4 Apr. 2018.

Editors, C W. *Fred Rogers' Widow Joanne, Chats with Closer about TV Legend's Legacy*. 16 Feb. 2018, www.pressreader.com/usa/closer-weekly/20180216/281603830918846. Accessed 4 Apr. 2018.

Merritt, J. *Saint Fred*. 22 Nov. 2015, www.theatlantic.com/politics/archive/2015/11/mister-rogers-saint/416838/. Accessed 4 Apr. 2018.

Wellons, N I. *Mrs. Rogers' Neighborhood.* 9 July 2001, articles.baltimoresun.com/2001-07-09/features/0107090232_1_fred-rogers-rogers-neighborhood-mister-rogers. Accessed 4 Apr. 2018.

Wellons, N I. *Mrs. Rogers' Neighborhood.* 9 July 2001, articles.baltimoresun.com/2001-07-09/features/0107090232_1_fred-rogers-rogers-neighborhood-mister-rogers/2. Accessed 4 Apr. 2018.

Cosgrove-Mather, B. *Mrs. Rogers Tells All -- Nicely.* 8 Oct. 2003, www.cbsnews.com/news/mrs-rogers-tells-all-nicely/. Accessed 4 Apr. 2018.

Neuhaus, C. *Fred Rogers Moves into a New Neighborhood—and So Does His Rebellious Son.* 15 May 1978, people.com/archive/fred-rogers-moves-into-a-new-neighborhood-and-so-does-his-rebellious-son-vol-9-no-19/. Accessed 4 Apr. 2018.

Rochman, S. *A Beautiful Neighbor.* 31 Dec. 2014, www.cancertodaymag.org/Pages/Winter2014-2015/Fred-Rogers-Mister-Rogers-Died-From-Stomach-Cancer-Taught-Children-Compassion.aspx. Accessed 4 Apr. 2018.

Editors, P G. *Josie Carey and WQED's Children's Corner.* 20 Dec. 2013, newsinteractive.post-gazette.com/thedigs/2013/12/20/josie-carey-and-wqeds-childrens-corner/. Accessed 4 Apr. 2018.

Editors, R C. *EARLY YEARS IN TELEVISION.* 2015, www.fredrogerscenter.org/about-us/about-fred/mister-rogers-neighborhood/early-years-in-television/. Accessed 4 Apr. 2018.

Editors, F R. *Beginnings.* 2018, www.fredrogers.org/about/beginnings/. Accessed 4 Apr. 2018.

Editors, T A. *Josie Carey, 73: Children's TV Pioneer.* 2012, www.emmys.com/news/josie-carey-73-childrens-tv-pioneer. Accessed 5 Apr. 2018.

Flecker, S A. *When Fred Met Margaret.* 2014, www.pittmed.health.pitt.edu/story/when-fred-met-margaret. Accessed 5 Apr. 2018.

Editors, N T. *M.B. McFarland, 83, A Child Psychologist.* 14 Sept. 1988, www.nytimes.com/1988/09/14/obituaries/mb-mcfarland-83-a-child-psychologist.html. Accessed 5 Apr. 2018.

Strachan, M. *The Best Argument For Saving Public Media Was Made By Mr. Rogers In 1969.* 16 Mar. 2017, www.huffingtonpost.com/entry/mr-rogers-pbs-budget-cuts_us_58ca8d6fe4b0be71dcf1d440. Accessed 5 Apr. 2018.

Bradberry, T. *How Emotional Intelligence Landed Mr. Rogers $20 Million.* 25 Sept. 2014, www.forbes.com/sites/travisbradberry/2014/09/25/how-emotional-intelligence-landed-mr-rogers-20-million/#6861d8924b63. Accessed 5 Apr. 2018.

Lewis, F. *African-American History Timeline: 1940 to 1949.* 8 Mar. 2017, www.thoughtco.com/african-american-history-timeline-1940-1949-45441. Accessed 5 Apr. 2018.

Abramovitch, S. *Oscar's First Black Winner Accepted Her Honor in a Segregated 'No Blacks' Hotel in L.A.* 19 Feb. 2015, www.hollywoodreporter.com/features/oscars-first-black-winner-accepted-774335. Accessed 5 Apr. 2018.

Mettler, K. *'We'Re Truly Sorry': Fla. Apologizes for Racial Injustice of 1949 'Groveland Four' Rape Case.* 19 Apr. 2017, www.washingtonpost.com/news/morning-mix/wp/2017/04/19/were-truly-sorry-after-68-years-florida-apologizes-for-racist-history-of-groveland-four/?utm_term=.d9a636c8bd16. Accessed 5 Apr. 2018.

Hiskey, D. *15 INTERESTING MR. ROGERS FACTS.* 19 Feb. 2013, www.todayifoundout.com/index.php/2013/02/15-interesting-mr-rogers-facts/. Accessed 5 Apr. 2018.

Editors, E T. *CHILDREN'S CORNER, THE.* 2013, www.emmytvlegends.org/interviews/shows/childrens-corner-the. Accessed 5 Apr. 2018.

Editors, N A. *Misterogers.* 2013, www.neighborhoodarchive.com/mrn/episodes/misterogers/index.html. Accessed 5 Apr. 2018.

Jackson, C. *The Importance of Sweaters and Sneakers in Mister Rogers' Neighborhood.* 20 Mar. 2017, www.rewire.org/pbs/sweaters-sneakers-rogers-neighborhood/. Accessed 5 Apr. 2018.

Editors, P S. *Watch Mister Rogers' Heart-Warming Message to His Grownup Fans.* 27 Feb. 2015, www.pbs.org/newshour/nation/watch-fred-rogers-heart-warming-final-message-grownup-fans. Accessed 5 Apr. 2018.

Editors, A. *Mister Rogers-Robert F Kennedy Assassination Special.* 17 Oct. 2017, archive.org/details/youtube-juwdeDzjVCQ. Accessed 5 Apr. 2018.

Editors, N R. *Walking The Beat In Mr. Rogers' Neighborhood, Where A New Day Began Together.* 11 Mar. 2016, www.npr.org/2016/03/11/469846519/walking-the-beat-in-mr-rogers-neighborhood-where-a-new-day-began-together. Accessed 5 Apr. 2018.

Editors, N A. *Episode 1065.* 2011, www.neighborhoodarchive.com/mrn/episodes/1065/index.html. Accessed 5 Apr. 2018.

Editors, B P. *Davis, Doris A. (1935-)*. 2016, www.blackpast.org/aaw/davis-doris-1935. Accessed 5 Apr. 2018.

Editors, N A. *Mayor Maggie*. 2011, www.neighborhoodarchive.com/mrn/characters/mayor_maggie/index.html. Accessed 5 Apr. 2018.

Editors, N A. *John Reardon (Character)*. 2011, www.neighborhoodarchive.com/mrn/characters/reardon/index.html. Accessed 5 Apr. 2018.

Editors, N A. *Episode 1739*. 2011, www.neighborhoodarchive.com/mrn/episodes/1739/index.html. Accessed 5 Apr. 2018.

Editors, N A. *Episode 1765*. 2012, www.neighborhoodarchive.com/mrn/episodes/1765/index.html. Accessed 5 Apr. 2018.

Demain, B. *How Mister Rogers Saved the VCR*. 9 Jan. 2012, mentalfloss.com/article/29686/how-mister-rogers-saved-vcr. Accessed 5 Apr. 2018.

Madrigal, A C. *The Court Case That Almost Made It Illegal to Tape TV Shows*. 10 Jan. 2012, www.theatlantic.com/technology/archive/2012/01/the-court-case-that-almost-made-it-illegal-to-tape-tv-shows/251107/. Accessed 5 Apr. 2018.

Long, M. G. (2015). *Peaceful Neighbor: Discovering the Countercultural Mister Rogers*. Westminster John Knox Press.

Lowenfish, L. (2009). *Branch Rickey: Baseball's Ferocious Gentleman*. U of Nebraska Press.

Free Books by Charles River Editors

We have brand new titles available for free most days of the week. To see which of our titles are currently free, click on this link.

Discounted Books by Charles River Editors

We have titles at a discount price of just 99 cents everyday. To see which of our titles are currently 99 cents, click on this link.

Made in the USA
Middletown, DE
09 October 2020

21533957R00024